Philosophy for children

From child to children

Once upon a time!

We must never lie!

From child to children

By: Bernardo Octaviano Pereira

This book belongs to:

____

I dedicate this work, firstly, to my parents who I love so much, to my teachers, to my dear aunts and to all my friends, may God bless you all infinitely!

Bernardo Octaviano Pereira

03/04/2024

Once upon a time, not far from here, in a village of woodcutters, where the majority lived by cutting down trees to survive, and they spent the whole day cutting down trees, which was used for various things;

In this village, there was also a very naughty, messy and, unfortunately, very lying little boy. He loved to play pranks on lumberjacks, interrupting their important tasks.

The little boy used to go to where the woodcutters were working and start shouting loudly, - Help is the wolf, help the wolf will get me; - Help is the wolf, help the wolf will get me;

The
woodcutters,
worried about
the boy's safety,
dropped
everything and
ran to save him.
However, when
they got there,

there was no wolf, and the boy laughed at the situation. The woodcutters, after giving serious scoldings, went back to work.

The other day the boy was there playing tricks on the woodcutters again, - And the wolf, help the wolf will get me, help;

Again, the woodcutters, worried about the boy's safety, abandoned their tasks and ran to help. However, when they arrived,

I didn't find any wolves, just the boy laughing at them. The scoldings were repeated, but the woodcutters returned to the arduous task of chopping firewood.

However, on another day, the boy, playing his usual games, started shouting again:

-Help is the wolf, the wolf is going to get me, help, only this time, to everyone's surprise, a real wolf appeared. The boy, in genuine despair, screamed for help.

Unfortunately, the woodcutters, suspicious of the previous lies, did not come to his aid, believing it was just another joke.

The wolf, without being restrained, ended up attacking the boy for real. The tragic lesson of this story is clear, Never lie, if you lie, and if one day you tell the truth, no one will believe you.

The tragic lesson of this story is clear: never lie. If you get used to lying, when you tell the truth, no one will believe you.

Sincerity is valuable and builds trust, while lying can have unexpected and sad consequences. May this fable inspire us to be honest in all situations

The end!